Spilling the Beans on

Blackbeard

and his murderous mateys

First published in 2000 by Miles Kelly Publishing,
Bardfield Centre, Great Bardfield, Essex CM7 4SL

Reprinted 2001

Printed in Italy

ISBN 1-902947-40-1

2468109753

Cover design and illustration: Inc
Layout design: GardnerQuainton

Spilling the Beans on Blackbeard

and his murderous mateys

by Martin Oliver

Illustrations   Mike Mosedale

About the Author

Martin Oliver has written over 20 fiction and non-fiction books for children. His interest in pirates started with watching *Captain Pugwash* cartoons and he would love to visit the Caribbean – purely for research purposes of course. He lives near the River Thames in southwest London with his wife and two young daughters.

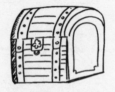

Contents

Mad, bad and dangerous to know

Mention the word 'pirate' and one name instantly springs to mind – Blackbeard! Even in the world of the bloodthirsty buccaneers' horrible habits and terrible tricks, he stands out as the cruellest, wickedest and downright baddest of them all.

But was he really as mad, bad and dangerous to know as everyone imagines? We put his reputation on the line and give you the low down on this low-down character. We'll also lift the lid on a whole host of fascinating facts that you may not know about Blackbeard. Read on as we *spill the beans* on why he threatened to set fire to an entire port for an old wooden chest, why he kept a specially-sharpened knife by his side at all times, what unusual role he gave his wives and why to some people he may not have been a pirate after all.

And what about Blackbeard's fellow pirates? If you've read about them in books or seen them in the movies, you'll be familiar with a world of peg-leg swashbucklers, of pet parrots, of grog drinking, buried treasure and a high old life on the high seas. But while some of the details might be based on the truth, we'll help to put you in the picture about what life was really like on the ocean waves. Our Rogues' Gallery features some of the cruellest captains of all time and we give you a true taste of life below decks. You can check out favourite terror tactics and even sample some rough justice...

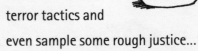

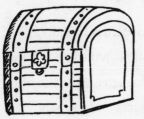

So, if you think you've got what it takes to keep up with the wicked ways and gruesome goings-on of Blackbeard and his fellow plundering pirates, be prepared to weigh anchor and set sail for the seven seas...

CHAPTER ONE

Pirate or Privateer?

Blackbeard lived during what some people (although not his victims) call the golden age of piracy. For many years, the seas around America had been crowded with merchant vessels piled high with cargoes from the continent. These treasures had attracted thousands of adventurers, rogues and ruffians who were keen to get their hands on these rich pickings by any means possible.

To help him stay ahead in this cut-throat world, Blackbeard had plenty of tricks up his sleeve and one of the cleverest was to claim that he wasn't a pirate at all – but a privateer. To discover just how clever his scheme was, why not see if you can spot the difference between a pirate and a privateer?

That's right, to the untrained eye – or to their victims – they were exactly the same but there was one vital difference between pirates and privateers. The difference was that privateers carried 'letters of marque'. These gave them legal authority to attack ships and were handed out by governments who used pirates as some sort of unofficial navy to fight their battles and attack other countries for them. What's more, as long as privateers didn't attack ships belonging to their own country, they couldn't be put on trial as pirates.

Did you know?

Apart from Blackbeard, one of the most famous privateers of all time was Sir Francis Drake. To the Spanish empire he was nothing but a common pirate but Queen Elizabeth I realised how useful he was and gave him letters of marque. Armed with permission from his queen, Drake had a right royal time attacking Spanish ships and towns. He returned home as a national hero, his ships' holds bulging with over £500,000 worth of plunder – a sum that would be worth about 100 times as much today.

Gruesome crewsomes

Whether you think he was a pirate or a privateer, there's no doubt that Blackbeard was one of the most feared pirate captains. However, he wasn't the first to spread terror on the high seas. Ever since peaceful sailors took to the sea they've not only had to survive everything the oceans could throw at them but they've also had to battle an even fiercer enemy.

Pirates, corsairs, sea rovers, filibusters, freebooters or buccaneers – whatever they were called, they came in all shapes and sizes and all had one aim in common – to spread terror on the seven seas. To help you survive an attack from these gruesome crewsomes, why not take a voyage back in time and keep a good lookout for our ferocious fact attacks.

GALLEY GANGS

When they sailed:
From 250 BC – AD 250.

Favourite haunts:
Around the Mediterranean and Arabian Seas.

Favourite targets:
Merchant ships carrying spices, grain and even slaves around

the Roman empire. They would also attack and loot any prosperous coastal towns or islands.

How to spot a Galley Gang:

These pirates were mainly Greek, Phoenician or Sicilian but they could be anyone who disliked the Roman empire.

Their favourite ships were long galleys rowed by slaves and with a battering ram at the front. They would use catapults or Greek fire to soften up their opponents before moving in for the kill with short swords and knives. Particularly crafty pirates used their oars to make their boat dip just before impact so their battering ram would hit their opponent's ship below the waterline.

Did you know?

One particular galley gang made a big mistake in 75 BC when

they captured a ship whose passengers included the future emperor, Julius Caesar. Furious at having his holiday plans spoiled, Caesar caused the pirates all sorts of problems.

1. First of all he complained when he found out how much the pirates were asking for his ransom – he thought it was much too low.

2. He constantly complained about the cramped conditions he was being kept in and wrote awful poems.

3. He didn't show much gratitude for being released unharmed. Shortly after being freed, he gathered an army and captured the pirates. He ordered that their throats should be cut and their bodies nailed to trees before he continued with his holiday on Rhodes.

No-good Norsemen

When they sailed:

From AD 780 – 1050.

Favourite haunts:

The North Sea, the Atlantic Ocean and the Baltic and Black Seas.

Favourite targets:

The no-good Norsemen weren't particularly fussy about their victims. They would attack the Irish, Saxons, Russians or anyone else who lived on the coasts that were within their range. These Viking pirates were quite happy to attack towns and farms but they were particularly keen on plundering Christian abbeys and churches.

How to spot no-good Norsemen:

The Norsemen sailed in oak longships that could be as much as

23 metres long. They had a pine mast with a single sail and were rowed by up to 100 crewmen. Vikings rarely fought battles at sea but anchored just offshore before heading inland. They wore armour and iron helmets and carried spears, swords and razor-sharp axes.

Did you know?

The name 'Viking' probably comes from the old English word for 'sea-raiding'. The Vikings were so terrifying that peaceful Christians wrote special prayers asking to be spared from them.

MEDIEVAL MANIACS

When they sailed:

From AD 1060 – 1500.

Favourite haunts:

The North Sea, the Irish Sea and the Atlantic Ocean.

Favourite targets:

English, French, German, Irish – basically, almost anyone who was unlucky enough to get within range. During this time, the seas were full of merchant ships carrying cargoes of coal, silk, linen, wine and spices that were easy prey for the medieval maniacs.

How to spot a medieval maniac:

Pirates sailed out from their bases in secluded coastal inlets and islands in a variety of small, fast ships known as cogs or round-ships. They fired arrows from long range then used swords, maces and daggers for hand-to-hand combat.

Did you know?

One of the most feared medieval maniacs had once been a monk. After a serious bit of monk-ey business, Eustace the Black Monk was outlawed for murder and ran away to sea. He sailed up and down the English Channel attacking first French boats then English boats. His opponents thought he was in league with the devil and certainly they had a devil of a time before they managed to track him down and chop off his head.

CORSAIR KILLERS

When they sailed:

From AD 1300 – 1800.

Favourite haunts:

The Mediterranean Sea.

Favourite targets:

It all depended on which type of corsair you were. The

Barbary corsairs, who were Muslims, and Christian corsairs were deadly enemies. When the Islamic religion began spreading westwards, leaders of Europe's Christian nations became concerned and they formed their own navies to control the countries and trade routes around the Mediterranean.

How to spot corsair killers:

All corsair galleys were around 50 metres long and were rowed by slaves. However, the galleys of most Barbary corsairs had one mast, a single cannon at the bow and a long battering ram. Their favourite tactic was to get their galley as close as possible to their opponents' boat, then heavily-armed pirates with scimitars, muskets and curved daggers would scramble aboard for hand-to-hand fighting.

Christian corsairs often had two or three masts and more cannons at the bow to port and starboard. Instead of taking on the Barbary corsairs at close quarters, the Christians preferred to use their cannons to blast opponents out of the water from a safe distance.

Did you know?

The most feared Muslim corsairs were the Greek brothers, Aruj and Khair-ed-din. They were nicknamed the Barbarossa brothers meaning 'red-beard' because of the colour of their hair. This dynamic duo ran rings around their Christian opponents and even when Aruj was killed, his brother Khair-ed-din lived to fight many more days and became the Admiral of the Turkish Fleet.

BRUTAL BUCCANEERS

When they sailed:

From AD 1500 – 1750.

Favourite haunts:

Mainly active within the Spanish Main – around the Caribbean islands and where North America meets South America.

Favourite targets:

Spanish galleons or anyone else returning with valuable cargo of gold, silver, spices or slaves from the Americas.

How to spot brutal buccaneers:

Over the years, buccaneers used all sorts of different ships. In the early days they launched surprise attacks from dugout canoes before turning to bigger and faster ships, including their favourite vessels – sloops. Occasionally they even commandeered Spanish galleons and other merchants' ships to turn against their former owners. To attack slow but heavily-armed ships, they preferred fast, manoeuvrable craft. After boarding a ship they relied on their cutlass, pistol and musket skills in close-quarter fighting.

Did you know?

Buccaneers got their name from the way in which they cooked

their meat. When the Spanish rulers of the Caribbean got fed up with the lawless adventurers who were attacking their citizens, they drove them out of the towns and into wild, jungle areas. Here they banded together, living in open-air camps and hunting for food. When they killed an animal, they cooked the meat and smoked it in a large wooden oven called a 'boucan'. The name – and the smell – stuck.

JUNK SKUNKS

When they sailed:

From AD 1700 – 1920.

Favourite haunts:

The Indian Ocean, the Straits of Malacca and the South China Sea.

Favourite targets:

English ships carrying cotton, tea and other cargoes from their empire plantations.

How to spot junk skunks:

Their ships were a dead giveaway. Generally they sailed in junks or fast Arab dhows. Junks varied in size from small ships to large, three-masters that could carry up to 30 cannons. These pirates were particularly feared for their fierce fighting with pistols, razor-sharp daggers and curved swords – not to mention their horrible habit of beheading prisoners on the spot.

Did you know?

Perhaps the most brutal pirate of the south seas was a woman. Qing Er Sou, or Madame Cheng as she was known, was happy enough to be a pirate's wife until her husband died in 1807. She must have learned a few tricks of the trade from him because she took control of his 50,000 men and spent the next three years carrying on where her husband had left off. Instead of going to the watery grave she deserved, she managed to buy a pardon from the Chinese government and died peacefully.

CHAPTER TWO

A life on the ocean waves

Becoming a pirate always looks like good swashbuckling fun in Hollywood movies, but if you think that a life on the high seas was plain sailing, you'll be in for a few surprises. It's not the sort of career you'd see advertized in any papers and most buccaneers didn't live long enough to make it into a family business, so why did people choose such a difficult and dangerous way of life in the first place? Was it because:

a) They were particularly suited to a life of crime?

b) They were bored?

c) They wanted to save their own lives?

Answer: All of them.

a) There's no doubt that some people had exactly the right character for piracy – they were cruel and greedy. Before becoming such a terrifying figure, Blackbeard was just a simple merchant seaman called Edward Teach who sailed out of Bristol. It was after joining the crew of a pirate captain called Hornigold that he impressed the captain with one of his truly horrible habits. Instead of waiting for victims to hand over their rings, Blackbeard devised a true short cut – he just chopped off their fingers. As a result, when Hornigold captured a large French vessel, he made Blackbeard captain and his partner-in-crime's career was launched.

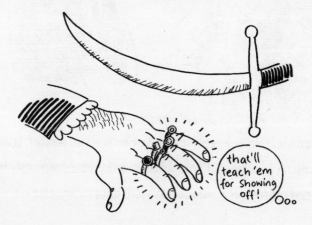

b) Major Stede Bonnet was one of the most unlikely pirates of all. After retiring from the army, he became a respectable plantation owner in Barbados. Famous for his extravagant clothes, he was bored with his life and turned to piracy. Unfortunately, he was just as bad at choosing his friends as he was his outfits and 1717 he joined Blackbeard's fleet. Blackbeard not only made fun of his dress sense, he also tricked him out of his ship. Left on his own, Bonnet was soon captured and was hung in 1718.

c) If you were unlucky enough to be captured by pirates, your future didn't look good. If you were wealthy, you'd probably be ransomed off for large amounts of gold but anyone else on board was usually given a simple choice – to die horribly or become a pirate. Not surprisingly, most people chose piracy.

Pirate positions

Having decided to embark on a career in piracy, there was no shortage of jobs. Leading such a dangerous life meant that pirates were always on the lookout for new blood. Which position could you have filled on a buccaneer's boat?

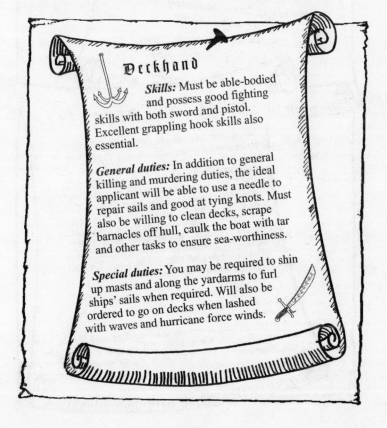

Deckhand

Skills: Must be able-bodied and possess good fighting skills with both sword and pistol. Excellent grappling hook skills also essential.

General duties: In addition to general killing and murdering duties, the ideal applicant will be able to use a needle to repair sails and good at tying knots. Must also be willing to clean decks, scrape barnacles off hull, caulk the boat with tar and other tasks to ensure sea-worthiness.

Special duties: You may be required to shin up masts and along the yardarms to furl ships' sails when required. Will also be ordered to go on decks when lashed with waves and hurricane force winds.

Lookout

Skills: Must have excellent eyesight, the ability to stay awake and be a good sailor.

General duties: to cling to the exposed rigging or crow's nest and keep a weather eye open for potential victims or enemies.

Special bonus: lookouts often enjoyed special rewards. If you sailed with George Lowther in 1720 and were the first crew member to spot the sail of a potential victim, you would receive the best pistol from that ship as a reward.

Ship's Carpenter

Skills: Must be good with their hands and also possess a strong stomach.

General duties: To keep up running repairs to the ship. You will be expected to perform a variety of general tasks such as sawing down planks and extracting nails from wood for use in other parts of the ship. The ability to mix up tar for waterproofing the hull is an added benefit. Applicants will not be expected to provide their own tools but having their own kit including hammer, chisels, pliers, saws and needles would be an advantage.

Special duties: To act as ship's surgeon when required. Your sawing skills will come in handy for amputating wounded limbs while rotten teeth can be chiselled out. Pliers and needles will be used to extract splinters or bullets while after amputating limbs, stumps will be dipped into tar to seal the wound.

Ship's Musician

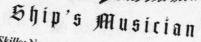

Skills: No musical ability required.

General duties: You will be a team player who can easily join in with other members of the on-board buccaneer band. Your main purpose will be to strike up such a terrible din that you frighten the living daylights out of your opponents before the fighting even begins.

Special notes: This position will suit applicants who are not as bloodthirsty or as greedy as their fellow crew. The successful applicant will not be expected to get involved with hand-to-hand fighting but will receive a smaller share of booty as a result.

Ship's Cook

Skills: Versatility and inventiveness more important than cooking ability.

General duties: While pirate crews aren't often fussy eaters, you will be expected to ensure that there is enough food for the crew to eat. The ability to be inventive when rustling up meals is essential – as is rat-catching ability.

Special notes: As cooks are not generally expected to fight during battles, this position would ideally suit an experienced sea-farer who may have lost a hand, arm or other limb during their career.

Ship's Gunner

Skills: to supervise the aiming, loading and firing of the ship's cannons.

General duties: During battle, you will be expected to direct your ship's broadsides of grapeshot and cannonballs at your opponents.

Special notes: If you are not already deaf you soon will be. Special bravery is also required as you are at greater risk of cannons exploding and from injuries caused by flying splinters.

Pirate power

Of course, the most important job of all was that of being a pirate captain. Captains in the navy or of merchant ships usually reached their rank through family connections but pirates had a completely different way of doing things. Pirate captains were elected by their crew and if they didn't measure up, they could just as easily be overthrown (or even thrown overboard).

Did you know?

Captain Edward England (who died in 1720) was one pirate captain who learned his lesson the hard way. He painted the Indian Ocean red in a series of successful attacks but when he let a merchant crew sail off in their sinking ship, his crew felt that he was going soft. Just to remind him of how true pirates behaved they set him adrift in the middle of the ocean in a small boat.

The result of this sort of pirate power was that the captain was often the fiercest, most terrifying person on board – a bit like your teacher really. When it came to keeping control of his motley crew, Blackbeard certainly led the way. In fact, when you find out how he treated his men, you'll probably never complain about your teachers again.

Shoot to thrill

Once when he was eating with his crew, Blackbeard blew out the candles and fired his pistols under the table without warning. One bullet hit the ship's master, Israel Hands, in his knee. When someone plucked up the courage to ask him why he'd done it, Blackbeard replied that "if I didn't shoot one of you now and then, you'd forget who I am".

Stinky surprise

Another of Blackbeard's horrible habits was to dare the toughest, meanest crew members to go below decks with him. Once they were in a small hold, he lit stink bombs of sulphur and tar. The stench was unbearable but while his pirates rushed for the fresh air, Blackbeard stayed below longer than anyone else.

Ship's survival

So now you've got some ideas about the different jobs that pirates did on board ship but before you sign up for the high life on the high seas, it's time to hold on to your hats (and your noses) as we give you a taste of life aboard a buccaneer's boat.

While it might seem fun, exciting and romantic at first glance, the words dull, deadly and filthy were actually closer to the mark. Of course you'd expect a pirate's life to be dangerous but the risks didn't always come from dodging cannonballs and cutlass thrusts. In fact, when we spill the beans on all the things you'd have to survive before you got within firing range of a prize, you might be surprised that any pirates lived long enough to attack anybody.

 WARNING!

The following section contains gruesome and graphic details. On no account should you give it to your little sister or read it before eating.

A taste of pirate life

To give you a true taste of pirate life, follow our simple steps below:

1. Take one pirate. Do not wash – ever.
Pirates rarely bathed or even changed their clothes. This wasn't a problem for one Barbary corsair, Rahmin Bin Gabr, who wore his clothes until they were rags and still married over 200 women. It didn't seem to stop Blackbeard's progress either as he had 14 wives. However on one occasion, a brave woman refused to marry him. She complained about his stench and said he was so smelly that she would sooner "kiss a pig".

2. Add plenty more pirates and squash together.
Pirate ships were always overcrowded. Pirates needed to outnumber the crew of any ships they attacked and so the crew would all have to eat and sleep together in cramped, damp conditions.

3. Place in filthy container.

Ships' holds would stink all year round while filthy bilge-water sloshed around below decks. In addition, there were no baths, basins or showers and toilets didn't even exist. Instead, there was a hole in the deck at the front of the ship called the 'heads'. After a visit, pirates just washed it down with sea water. In hot weather, the stench would have been unimaginable.

4. Accompany life on board with a diet of filthy water and revolting food.

That's right – if you think school dinners are bad, you'd never survive as a pirate. Buccaneers were anything but fussy eaters.

Fresh food ran out quickly on a voyage and salted meat wasn't an appetizing alternative. Pirates nicknamed dried meat 'junk' which was the name they also gave to bits of old rope. Sometimes fresh meat came in the most surprising shapes – ship's biscuit was infested with worms and weevils, while rats were often served up as a delicacy.

5. Soak in cold saltwater, bake in the hot sun and stew for months at a time.

Pirate voyages could last for months on end in the dangerous Caribbean waters. Bad weather would lead to waves breaking over the decks soaking the crew in sea water while hot tropical sunshine would bake the crew and their battered boat.

6. Wash down with large amounts of rum and other alcoholic drink.

Pirates were big drinkers. While they were cruising around looking for victims, they would often spend all day and night drinking. One particularly popular drink was known as 'Kill Devil'. This rum cocktail packed an extra punch thanks to its secret ingredient – gunpowder.

Chef's recommendation:

To savour the full flavour, take in deep breaths and savour the unmistakeable pirate aroma.

Deadly diseases

The pirate lifestyle was hardly a recipe for a long, healthy life and diseases often wiped out as many as half a ship's crew before the end of the voyage. As you might expect, pirates came up with their own kill or cure solution to this problem. To toughen up new recruits, they would leave them in a town or island where a particular disease was running riot. After a couple of months, they'd come back and pick up the now 'seasoned' survivors.

How can you tell if you're about to come down with a deadly disease? Try your hand with a bit of on-board medicine and see if you can match the disease to the symptoms.

1. Scurvy

2. Malaria

3. Yellow fever

4. Jaundice

5. Gangrene

a) Highly contagious disease. High temperatures producing fevers and bad dreams. Often fatal.

b) Cut or wound becoming infected through lack of cleanliness. Blood poisoning causing pain, fever and rapid death. Only known cure – amputation.

c) A lack of vitamins from fresh fruit causing teeth and hair to fall out, gums to go rotten and limbs to break and twist.

d) Highly contagious disease. Symptoms include fever and massive vomiting leading to death.

e) Skin turns yellow as a result of alcohol poisoning. Leads to a long lingering death.

Answers:
1.c, 2.a, 3.d, 4.e, 5.b.

Killer crew members

Even if you managed to survive revolting recipes, deadly diseases and treacherous seas, there was still one other danger you would have to face – your killer crewmates. Not surprisingly, long boring voyages with a crowd of heavily armed, heavy drinking crewmen didn't make for a quiet, peaceful time.

Gambling was one of the few activities pirates could enjoy on board – and it was one that led to many fights. One of the pirates' other favourite pastimes could also turn nasty. Mock trials or pantomimes were extremely popular. Buccaneers would take it in turns to stage elaborate scenes in which they were caught, put on trial and sentenced to death. Unfortunately, on one occasion, one of the pirates on trial got so carried away that he threw bombs at the 'jury' and attacked his prosecuting pirate with a sword.

As if that wasn't enough to worry about, buccaneers also used to draw up strict rules with even stricter punishments for anyone who broke them. These rules were called 'articles' and before a crew member could set sail, he would have to swear allegiance to them over an axe. Would you dare break them?

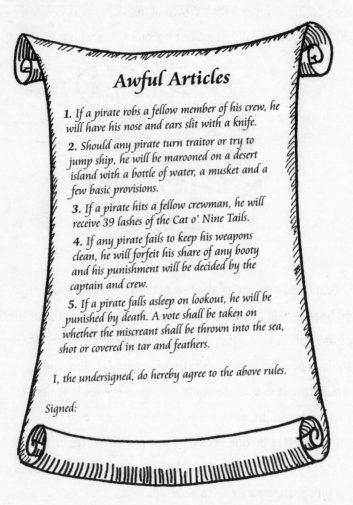

Awful Articles

1. If a pirate robs a fellow member of his crew, he will have his nose and ears slit with a knife.

2. Should any pirate turn traitor or try to jump ship, he will be marooned on a desert island with a bottle of water, a musket and a few basic provisions.

3. If a pirate hits a fellow crewman, he will receive 39 lashes of the Cat o' Nine Tails.

4. If any pirate fails to keep his weapons clean, he will forfeit his share of any booty and his punishment will be decided by the captain and crew.

5. If a pirate falls asleep on lookout, he will be punished by death. A vote shall be taken on whether the miscreant shall be thrown into the sea, shot or covered in tar and feathers.

I, the undersigned, do hereby agree to the above rules.

Signed:

Congratulations. If you've survived awful articles, beaten off deadly diseases and can stand the noxious niffs of a buccaneer's boat, then you might just be ready for the most dangerous part of all – to mount a real-life pirate attack.

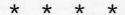

CHAPTER THREE

Pirates Ahoy!

The captain of the merchant vessel was nervous. He had doubled the lookouts and increased the punishment for any member of his crew found asleep at his post. After loading up

with a valuable cargo of tea and brandy they had set a course away from the Caribbean and were sailing north towards the Carolinas.

The port had been buzzing with rumours and was full of

ugly-looking characters who would sell details of their planned voyage for the price of a bottle of rum. That's why they had slipped anchor during the night and sailed away when the port was quiet. They had enjoyed good weather but even with the wind behind them their vessel was slow and heavy in the water. Every night the captain and his officers checked their cannons and muskets.

"Keep your eyes peeled," he had barked. "You know what you're looking for."

His crew had nodded and murmured. They knew the danger signs – small, manoeuvrable craft that quickly appeared over the horizon. However, so far the voyage had been uneventful.

They had nearly completed their voyage and the captain could tell that his men were beginning to relax and look forward to spending their wages on shore. Even the officers had started talking about feeling the ground beneath their feet once more. The captain was completing his daily entry into his logbook when suddenly, there was a shout from the crow's nest – "Sail ahoy. Starboard bow".

Trying to calm his pounding heart, the captain quickly produced his telescope. Where was it? Could the lookout have made a mistake – it was all too easy to confuse a distant sail with a whale, a cloud or even an island? There was a pause that seemed to last forever before the shout came again – "Sail ahoy, skipper".

The captain trained his telescope on the ship. It was a large schooner – manoeuvrable and approaching fast. She was riding high, not weighed down by cargo and the decks seemed empty. The captain looked up at the rigging and his heart soared. There it was, clear as day – the British flag flying high.

He was about to shout the good news to his crew when he suddenly noticed movement. Another flag was being run up. Could it be? Surely not. The captain's blood seemed to freeze in his veins. There it was – the most terrifying sight on the high seas – Blackbeard's flag!

BLACKBEARD

Terror tactics

It's hard now to imagine just how terrifying the sight of a pirate's flag could be. In fact, a Jolly Roger flying from a mast could turn the bravest crewman's legs to jelly, put any passengers into a screaming panic and make the captain think about giving up without a fight – which was exactly what pirates wanted.

It wasn't a question of cowardice – more a question of common sense. Even the toughest pirates like Blackbeard weren't stupid. After all, why should they risk death (or even worse, injury) by splinters, grapeshot, gunshots or cutlass thrusts if there was a chance of capturing their plunder without a battle.

As a result, the pirates' favourite plan of attack was to make sure their victims were too scared to put up a fight. They came up with their own terror tactics to ensure that when they ran up the Jolly Roger their opponents ran up the white flag.

HOISTING THE JOLLY ROGER

Blackbeard was one of the masters of these terror tactics and by flying his flag, he was following a long and dishonourable tradition that dated back to the early days of piracy. Viking raiders often hoisted pennants with ravens of their god Odin while the Barbary corsairs also got into the act by flying red flags. The French described them as *joli rouge* and it is thought that this is where the name Jolly Roger comes from. Another suggestion is that the name came from the old English nickname for the devil – Old Roger – which gives you an idea of what sailors thought of pirates.

While no one is entirely sure how the Jolly Roger got its name, what is sure is that by the 1700's, all self-respecting buccaneers flew a flag and individual captains often designed their own unique versions.

The standard Jolly Roger

Edward England was the pirate captain who flew the flag that everyone thinks of as the Jolly Roger. His unmistakeable flag showed the death's head and bones on a black background as warning to his opponents that he would fight to the death.

The triple Jolly Roger

The long triangular flag of Christopher Condent was three times as terrifying. This pirate captained the *Dragon* and he terrorized the Red Sea in 1719, seizing gold and spices. Eventually, he married a relative of the governor of Réunion and after retiring from piracy, he lived peacefully in St Malo.

CHRISTOPHER CONDENT

Blood-red banner

One glance at Christopher Moody's flag would do more than just shiver a few timbers. In addition to the skull and

CHRISTOPHER MOODY

crossbones, his flag contained an hourglass to warn victims that their time was running out and the raised sword and red background was a sign that blood would be spilt.

Scarlet skeleton

Edward Low was a particularly cruel pirate who sailed around the Americas' east coast in the 1720s. He enjoyed spilling blood so much that his flag showed a blood-red skeleton.

Heart attack

As you might expect, Blackbeard's unique flag was one of the most scary and sinister of the lot. It flew above his ship, *Queen Anne's Revenge*, and made a truly diabolical display showing the skeleton of a devil and a red bleeding heart.

FEARSOME FASHION

If the sight of a Jolly Roger wasn't enough to make you turn tail and run for your life, one good look at a motley crew of buccaneers might be enough to convince you to surrender. Armed to the teeth and wearing filthy rags, they would scream and shout to create an even more terrifying impression.

However, while movies seemed to show pirates with wooden legs and sharp hooks in place of hands, the reality was that able-bodied pirates were more likely to succeed at sea. Find out if you'd be a fashion-victim with our terrible trio of pirates who certainly knew how to dress to kill.

1. Captain John Rackham was one of the most colourful and successful buccaneers. He was nicknamed 'Calico Jack' after his habit of wearing bright, colourful trousers and spread terror around the Bahamas until, in November 1720, his final attempt to cut a dash was brought to an end by a British privateer.

2. French privateer, François le Clerc who was active in 1553-1554, was almost as famous for his nickname as his buccaneering exploits. Called *Jambe de Bois* (wooden leg) by his crew, he was actually one of the few peg-leg pirates to have a successful career attacking Spanish ships off Puerto Rico and the port of Santiago de Cuba.

3. When it came to fearsome fashion, one buccaneer blew all the others out of the water. Blackbeard didn't just act the part

of a cruel captain, he looked the part too. Of all the people you wouldn't want to meet in the day (let alone on a dark night) Edward Teach would have been that man. Blackbeard was gigantic, with hands reaching down below his knees – but that was just for starters.

If looks could kill, one glance at Blackbeard's awesome outfit would have been fatal.

Teach always sported black clothes, a colour that was associated with the devil. What's more, he kept them on always until they were ragged and filthy.

He grew an enormous beard which he curled into rats'-tails and to which he added pretty silk ribbons. To add to the lethal look, he stuck lighted fuses in his hair so it looked like clouds of smoke and flames were shooting out of his head.

As a final touch, Blackbeard always went into battle with six pistols strapped across his chest and a razor-sharp cutlass in his hand.

ACTING THE PART

Perhaps the most effective terror tactic was the buccaneers' reputation for cruelty. In fact, one bunch of 19th-century marauding murderers was so scary that their name became part of the English language. The awful exploits of the Bugis around Sumatra and New Guinea so terrified English sailors that they called them 'bogeymen' which means 'horrible creatures'.

There's no doubt that pirates were a very cruel bunch who enjoyed inflicting pain on their victims but they probably didn't just do it for kicks. It was handy for buccaneers to have a rotten reputation because if sailors thought that by fighting they risked death by a thousand cuts (or worse), they might just give up without putting up a struggle.

Of course, that didn't mean some pirate captains and crews didn't dream up some particularly gruesome treatments for their captives. When it came to cruelty, there were plenty of rivals willing to give Blackbeard a run for his money, as you'll discover when you check out our Rogues' Gallery of killer captains.

Roche Brasiliano (active in the 1670s)

This Dutch captain was notorious for having a particularly hot temper. His speciality was barbecuing his prisoners alive.

François l'Olonnais (active in the 1660s)

He hated the Spanish so much that he once cut a Spanish captain's heart out while the victim was still alive and regularly beheaded any prisoners. He eventually got his just desserts when he was captured by native American braves who hacked him to death and burned the remains.

Edward Low (active in the 1710s)

This cruel captain displayed an even more terrifying taste in cookery. He once cut off and toasted one victim's lips and on another occasion he sliced the ear off one captain, then garnished it with salt and pepper before forcing the man to eat it.

Edward Morgan (1635–1688)

He was one of the cruellest buccaneers of all time. He led a series of lightning attacks against Spanish settlements on the Caribbean islands, killing and looting as he went. His favourite trick to get Spanish captives to cough up the whereabouts of their hidden treasure was to tie individuals down and put heavy stones on them. Morgan managed to escape justice in the end. As most of his victims were Spanish, he became a British hero and was rewarded by being made governor of Jamaica.

CRUEL CREWS

Some pirates were determined not to let their captains hog all the headlines and they tried to live up to their cut-throat reputation. Which of the following fates actually befell unfortunate victims?

a) They were sewn up in a sail and thrown overboard.

b) They were made to walk the plank.

c) They were locked in the hold of a sinking ship.

d) They were hoisted from the mast then dropped on to the deck.

e) They were made to walk between the crew who lined up to punch and stab at them.

Answer: all of them – except **b**.

You've read about it hundreds of times but in reality it is thought that pirates never made victims walk the plank at cutlass-point. There is only one recorded mention of this type of treatment dating from 1769. It was in this year that a captured pirate, George Ward, confessed that during a mutiny, some sailors who stayed loyal to the captain were made to walk the plank. However, it is now thought that he may have just made it up.

Pirate attack

If terror tactics didn't work, there was no alternative but to stand and fight. However, as you might imagine, when it came to attacking, pirates liked to fight dirty.

RULES OF
PIRATE ATTACKS

1. Win at all costs.
2. Er, that's it – there are no more rules.

Pirate attacks have often hit the headlines. Glance through the stories uncovered by our roving reporter – do you think you would have withstood some of the dirty tricks buccaneers had up their sleeves?

SURPRISE, SURPRISE!

In a poll carried out by this newspaper, pirate captains have come clean about the tactics they use when attacking. 100% of respondents confirmed that they preferred to hit and run rather than risk a straight fight. The majority admitted that they had often used small canoes or boats to row up to moored boats and attack their crew in the night. Over 75% also said that they had flown fake merchants' flags but we could find no evidence that anyone had ever dressed up in women's clothing to fool their opponents.

PUMPKIN PIRATES

How could some drums and a wagon-load of pumpkins help Henry Morgan escape the Spanish navy? We spill the beans with our exclusive scoop. His explosive story begins one night a few weeks ago on the Venezuelan coast. Captain Morgan takes up the story himself.

"We were sacking the city of Maracaibo when one of my guards shouted a warning. Three Spanish warships had appeared blocking the harbour – and our escape route. We couldn't outgun or outrun them so the only way to escape was to outsmart them. I kept racking my brains but it wasn't until I saw a merchant ship, some drums and the pumpkins that I knew we could do it."

The pirate captain confirmed that they packed the ship with tar, sulphur and gunpowder to make a floating firebomb but that still left a problem – if they didn't do something clever, the Spanish would spot the fireboat in time to escape. Only now can we reveal the ingenuity of the solution to this problem.

The pirates used Indian drums to make fake cannons and put the pumpkins on top of dummies so they would look like pirates. Disguised to look like Morgan's boat, they sailed the ship towards the Spanish. In the darkness, the Spanish were fooled. They fired a broadside and the fore boat blew up, taking its attackers with it.

Awful ammunition!

One pirate captain who wished to remain anonymous has confirmed his use of awful ammunition. Claiming it had been a 'last resort' when he was running short of ammunition, he ordered his men to load up their cannons with gold coins.

"The result was awesome," admitted the captain. "And once we had captured our prize, I ordered the surgeon to remove the gold from the victim's bodies."

Friend or foe?

We caught up with Welsh pirate, Howell Davis, after a week-long binge that was held to celebrate his sacking of a Gambian fort. Captain Davis explained how he managed to steal huge amounts of gold bars and ivory from the supposedly invincible building.

"I knew my impersonations would come in handy," Davis explained, clutching a bottle of brandy. "We sailed right into the port as bold as brass and I then called in to see the commander of the fort. He was worried about a Welsh buccaneer but I fooled him into thinking I was a trader from Liverpool. It worked so well that he invited me and my crew for dinner. Once we were inside the fort, we produced our pistols and took the loot."

Bonny buccaneers

There was still one surprise that some buccaneers managed to spring on unsuspecting sailors. If you thought that to be a bloodthirsty, cut-throat buccaneer you had to be a man – you'd be wrong. Some of the toughest, bravest pirates of all have turned out to be women, as you'll discover when you check out our bonny buccaneers below.

Grace O'Malley was an Irishwoman from a noble family who led a whole fleet of pirates off the Irish coast in the 1560s. She was well-known for cutting her hair short and she soon had her enemies tearing their hair out. After 40 years of piracy, she sailed into an English port and personally negotiated a peace deal with another woman who also had short hair but wasn't short of courage – Queen Elizabeth I.

The crew of the Spanish ship, the *Maria*, thought they were safe when a storm drove them into the shelter of Falmouth Bay, Cornwall. Anchored below the home of the respectable Killigrew family, they let down their guard. Unfortunately, it proved a costly mistake as the lady of the house boarded the ship with her servants. The Spanish were then thrown overboard and the ship's cargo sold at a handsome profit.

Deadly duo, Mary Read and Anne Bonny, were both captured by 'Calico' Jack Rackham after they had run away to sea. They persuaded him to let them join his crew and were soon well-known for their bravery in battle. When Calico Jack was finally captured in 1720, the bonny buccaneers were only overpowered after a fierce fight while their captain was found hiding below decks. Sympathy wasn't their strong suit either – when Rackham was taken away to be hung, Anne Bonny said "if he had fought like a man, he need not have been hanged like a dog".

CHAPTER FOUR

Treasure Tales

Why did Blackbeard and his cut-throat cronies spend months crowded into a filthy boat risking a long, lingering death? The answer is of course because of the riches that were available on the high seas. Booty, plunder, loot – whatever you call it, that's what the buccaneers were after and they would go to great lengths to make sure they got it.

Did you know?

Buccaneers had some ingenious ways to make sure no one hid any valuables from them. One of their terrible tricks was to force passengers to drink a cocktail of rich spices and salty sea water until they were sick. As they emptied the contents of their stomachs, the crew would check to see if they had swallowed any jewels or treasure.

Another wicked way to make sure they got their greedy hands on the goodies was to throw any captured passengers and crew overboard. The pirates would then only rescue anyone who held up something valuable. If you weren't wealthy, all you could afford was a one-way ticket to Davy Jones's locker.

Lifting the lid on pirate treasure

Think of pirate treasure and what comes to mind? Most people imagine piles of glittering jewels and chests spilling over with doubloons, silver ingots and gold bars but the truth about pirate treasure was actually quite different.

There was no way of knowing exactly what cargo a ship was carrying so pirates couldn't afford to be choosy. Whether they attacked on land and sea, they took whatever came their way. As a result, buccaneers' booty came in all sorts of surprising shapes and sizes.

1. Some buccaneers lassoed a quick profit by rounding up cattle on inland raids. They would then sell the meat and hides to passing ships.

2. Many pirates traded in human cargo. For hundreds of years, the slave trade proved particularly valuable to the pirates. Rich prisoners could also be ransomed to boost the pirates' profits while replacement crew-members could be recruited from captured seafarers.

3. Cargoes of sugar, tobacco and even linen and coal were popular as they could be disposed of quickly and easily.

4. Ropes, sails and charts were always stripped from captured prizes. Sometimes even whole ships were taken. Blackbeard's vessel had been a French merchantman's before it was captured and renamed the *Queen Anne's Revenge*.

5. With so much danger from deadly diseases, medical supplies were almost as precious as gold and jewels. In 1718, Blackbeard threatened to set the port of Charleston ablaze if a complete medical chest was not sent out to him immediately. As usual, Blackbeard's negotiating skills won the day.

Plunder or blunder?

Perhaps the most vital ingredient for a pirate was being lucky – a quality that was in short supply for the unfortunate individuals below.

1. One group of pirates from Hastings paid the ultimate penalty for an act of piracy. In 1769 they were hanged – for stealing 60 hats.

2. In 1681, one crew of booty blunderers actually captured the *Santa Rosario* with a cargo of 400 silver ingots.

Unfortunately, they thought the silver was tin and threw the whole lot overboard.

However, while some buccaneers didn't enjoy the luck of the draw, others hit the jackpot when it came to plunder. We spill the beans on the top four treasure-takers.

CAPTAIN AVERY

The prize for capturing the biggest booty in one attack goes to the English pirate, John Avery. Avery's luck was certainly in when he spotted the aptly named *Exceeding Treasure* that belonged to the Grand Moghul of India. Weighed down with gold bars, silver coins, jewels and silks, it was a sitting duck for the prowling buccaneers who became the richest pirates on the Spanish Main overnight.

CAPTAIN BARTHOLOMEW 'BLACK BART' ROBERTS

In just four years between 1718 and 1722, Captain Roberts and his crew lived the high life on the high seas. Between them they managed to capture over 400 ships – enough to make every single member of his crew filthy rich.

CAPTAIN HENRY MORGAN

A series of raids on Spanish colonies in the Caribbean made the marauding Morgan and his brutal buccaneers extremely wealthy. They even had enough cash left over to pay out generous compensation. If you lost an eye, you'd receive 100 Spanish dollars. To make up for a missing leg pirates would get 600 dollars, and if you were in double trouble with no legs, you'd receive 1800 dollars to cushion the blow.

BLACKBEARD

Somewhere at the top of the pirate rich list was Blackbeard. Although no one can be sure exactly how much booty he amassed, during one particularly successful spell, he managed to capture four ships, set a port on fire and loot several plantations – all within two months.

Slicing and dicing

Trying to divide up their ill-gotten gains could often lead to another battle amongst greedy buccaneers. To prevent this sort of behaviour, pirates would sometimes agree to a division of spoils. In 1720, Captain George Lowther's crew came up with a strict way of splitting up their loot. Here's how they sliced and diced it.

Captain's portion	2 shares
Ship's master	1½ shares
Doctor/mate/gunner	1¼ shares
Crew	1 share

Pirate Ports

After capturing a prize and dividing up the booty, most pirates had only one thing on their mind – spending their ill-gotten gains. Apart from gambling, there was nothing to do with the money on board and there was no point risking your life if they couldn't go out and enjoy it.

As a result, there was nothing that Blackbeard and his fellow buccaneers liked better than carousing in bars, spending money on the finest clothes and losing fortunes over gambling or women. However, as most pirates were seen as little more than common criminals, they faced a major problem. Where could they enjoy their plunder without worrying about being caught and put on trial?

Just imagine that you are a bloodthirsty buccaneer in the 1700s. You've just captured a great prize and the loot is starting to burn a hole in your pocket. You've already been celebrating by drinking the boat dry and now you can feel your eyes closing. As you fall asleep amongst your snoring crewmen, you start dreaming of a pirate paradise – a safe haven that might well look like this.

A sheltered natural harbour with batteries of cannons guarding the port from any pirate-chasers or navies.

Quayside full of warehouses, piled high with plunder.

Naturally, there would be merchants to haggle with over prices and to trade your booty with.

If you wanted the finest clothes, there'd be an excellent choice of tailors.

You'd find carpenters to repair battered ships, doctors to repair battered bodies and goldsmiths for that glittering prize.

There would of course be hundreds of slaves and women.

You'd find hundreds of taverns and inn-keepers who are happy to stay open all hours and provide drinking and gambling facilities.

Above all else, there would be no police or army who might like to put a stop to your amusements such as taking pot-shots at slaves or anyone who refused you a drink.

Sounds too good to be true? In fact, pirates set up safe havens in many ports around the world, including the Scilly Isles and St Mary's Island near Madagascar. However, perhaps the biggest, liveliest and most wicked pirate paradise was the infamous Port Royal that was found on the Caribbean island of Jamaica – and which exactly matches the description above.

At its height, over 6,000 pirates and slaves flocked to what was one of the richest towns in the world. However, Port Royal's heyday was short-lived. In June 1692, an earthquake shook the buildings to their foundations. As the inhabitants ran for their lives, a colossal tidal wave then smashed through the port taking most of the buildings with it.

Some people claimed it was a punishment from God. Whether that's true or not, it's certain that Port Royal's reputation as a pirate paradise was over forever.

Treasure tales

If you were particularly successful like Blackbeard or just downright lucky like Captain Avery you could easily find yourself the proud owner of vast amounts of booty. It might seem like your problems were all over but in fact they were just beginning.

For a start, how could you dispose of your ill-gotten gains? In the days of the buccaneers, there were no banks where you could deposit your loot for sake-keeping. Even if you were as strong as Blackbeard, you'd be wise not to trust your fellow pirates too much and if you left it around to be robbed, you wouldn't find much help to get it back.

Most people think that the pirates came up with a solution to this problem – by burying their treasure. In fact, more buried treasure was hidden by people running away from pirates than was actually buried by pirates themselves – but this hasn't stopped stories springing up about legendary hoards of plunder just waiting to be discovered.

As one of the most successful pirates of all time, Blackbeard captured huge amounts of treasure – none of which has been discovered. Treasure-seekers believe that it must be buried in the Caribbean or North America but no one knows for sure as Blackbeard went to his grave claiming that it was a secret only he and the devil shared.

Blackbeard's booty isn't the only pirate plunder that people have tried – and failed – to find. The tiny Cocos Island is rumoured to hide three hidden treasure troves but none has ever been unearthed.

Perhaps there *are* hidden hoards of glittering jewels and gold bullion carefully hidden underground or perhaps it is just another pirate trick. Could Blackbeard and his band of buccaneers have simply spent all their ill-gotten gains and started the rumours of buried treasure to have the last laugh?

*   *   *   *

CHAPTER FIVE

Blackbeard's last stand

By the late 1710s, Blackbeard and his band of fellow buccaneers were at the height of their power. For years, they had enjoyed their reign of terror and they had never been so rich, so successful and so feared. Yet, the tide was beginning to turn against them as seafaring nations stopped fighting each other and began to send well-armed ships to sea to fight the pirates instead.

As one of the most ruthless pirates of the age, Blackbeard was top of the buccaneer-buster's hit list, but putting him out of business was far from plain sailing. It was the year 1718 and Blackbeard had been enjoying a particularly purple patch in his piracy career. His opponents knew that he would never give up without a fight...

The Pamlico River in North Carolina was proving to be a happy hunting ground for Blackbeard and he sailed up and down looting ships and plantations along the way. As a last resort, the local people called for help from the governor of the neighbouring colony of Virginia and so it was that Lieutenant Robert Maynard of the HMS *Pearl* found himself anchoring his ship opposite Ocracoke Inlet, just a few hundred yards away from his rival's hideout...

As night fell, Lieutenant Maynard called his officers together. Despite their calm appearance he could sense the tension in the air.

"What shall we do, sir?"

Maynard already had a plan of action. "Double your lookouts and break out the guns. We need to stay alert, who knows what the old rogue will do."

"Aye, aye sir," came the reply and the officers left Maynard's cabin to instruct their men. For the next few hours, Maynard lay awake and alert. Every creak of the ship's wooden hull or noise from the rigging seemed to echo in his ears. A loud knock had Maynard grasping his pistol and springing to the door. He accompanied the first mate on to the deck.

"Listen," he said and pointed across the water. Maynard strained his ears. There it was – the sound of singing and carousing. "I can't believe it," he muttered. "The old ruffian's drinking. Well, he'd better enjoy tonight, it will be his last one on Earth."

While Blackbeard and his men drank and caroused the night away, the crew of HMS *Pearl* dozed fitfully. By first watch at dawn, a light mist slowly began to clear. Moored just a few hundred yards away, Maynard could see his enemy's ship the *Queen Anne's Revenge*.

"Fire a shot across his bows," he barked. "We'll give him a chance to surrender."

Gunners scuttled to ram a cannonball down the gaping mouth of the cannon. When they were ready, the command to fire came. There was a loud bang and water spouted up near the bows of the pirate ship. Through his telescope Maynard watched as the ship's crew slowly came to life.

Never before had he seen a more terrifying bunch. With cutlasses in their teeth and ragged clothes bulging with pistols and muskets, they swarmed into positions all over the ship. Then, he saw a dark shadow and a huge figure appeared on the deck. Brandishing pistols in either hand he aimed at the ships and roared out, "Damnation seize my soul if I give a quarter or take any from you!"

"If it's a fight you're after, you've got it!" Maynard shouted back in reply. He turned to his officer and yelled commands for his crew to load their guns and prepare for battle. On the pirate ship, Blackbeard ran up his black flag, weighed anchor and headed straight for the English ships.

With the help of a strong current, the *Queen Anne's Revenge* was soon bearing down on them. The English ships panicked and fired off a couple of ragged broadsides. Still the pirates came closer and were soon in firing range. Maynard saw Blackbeard whipping up his men into a fury. BOOM! BOOM! BOOM! Deadly rounds of shots ripped across the river.

Both ships rocked and as the smoke cleared, Maynard could see the damage. The pirates' aim had been deadly. Dying men littered his deck and their groans filled the air. Up above, he could see their sails were in tatters and the deck was stained with blood.

"Get everyone below," yelled Maynard with a sinking heart. He knew that they couldn't afford to take any more casualties from another broadside but that with his crew below decks, Blackbeard could easily escape.

From his cabin, Maynard watched as Blackbeard's ship changed course. Instead of making for the open sea and freedom, they were heading straight for them. Maynard's heart began pounding – Blackbeard was obviously going in for the kill, but his own crew wasn't going to roll over and die.

Within minutes, the screaming pirates came closer. They hurled grappling hooks at the rigging and the two ships were dragged closer together. Maynard looked around at his remaining crew who were nervously clutching their muskets and swords. "Hold your fire, men," he hissed. "Blackbeard thinks we're finished but we can give him the fright of his miserable, murdering life. Wait until they're on board – NOW!"

The English crew charged above deck, firing a deadly volley as they went. Taken by surprise, the buccaneers were driven back. Maynard lead the charge and found himself eyeball-to-eyeball with Blackbeard. The huge pirate raised his pistol – and missed. Seizing his moment, Maynard drew his pistol and fired.

The huge pirate roared in pain then swung his cutlass. It shattered Maynard's weapon but before he could swing again a knife slashed him across the throat. Still Blackbeard fought on like a demon, firing and swinging his cutlass but the English had the upper hand. Abandoned by his men, Blackbeard was surrounded until at last he lay dying on the deck.

The battle was over. Maynard and his men gathered around the corpse of their giant enemy. When they counted Blackbeard's wounds, they discovered he had been shot five times and stabbed in almost twenty places. With one final blow, Maynard cut the pirate's head off and hung it from the bow of his ship as a grisly warning.

Unhappy endings

Blackbeard's death spelt the beginning of the end for the buccaneers and sparked a whole series of unhappy endings for his fellow pirates.

Some pirates died as they had lived and Captain Bartholomew 'Black Bart' Roberts was another pirate who went out with a bang. With his ship, *Royal Fortune*, weighed down with treasure and with his crew drunk on stolen brandy, he decided to stand and fight the crew of the English frigate HMS *Swallow*. In an epic struggle, both sides blew bits out of each other with broadsides of cannon and musket fire until a bullet hit Bart in the neck, killing him instantly.

For those pirates who survived any sea battles, there was nowhere to run onshore. If they were captured, the buccaneers were given the same sort of treatment they had dished out to their victims and could look forward to some very rough justice. Few pirates were shown any mercy, their only choices were:

1. To be hung, drawn and quartered.

2. To be beheaded.

3. To be hung until they were dead then have their bodies kept in cages.

4. To be tied to a stake and drowned by the incoming tide.

For those that escaped justice, few enjoyed a long, rich retirement. Inn-keepers were quite happy to live off a pirate's loot and then sell him into slavery as soon as his money ran out. Even the richest pirate of them all, Captain Avery, who had proved to be more than a match for the crew of the *Exceeding Treasure* was outwitted by merchants back at his home port of Bristol. He was swindled out of his booty and is believed to have died in poverty in Devon.

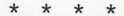

Blackbeard's last stand

Brave, cruel, greedy and ruthless – if you name the perfect ingredients to make a pirate, you'll now know that Blackbeard had them all plus a few extra ones thrown in for good measure. His legendary last stand ensured that his legend lives on hundreds of years after his death. For anyone brave or foolish enough to try and track down his missing plunder, there's one word of warning: Blackbeard is rumoured to have left his wives behind to guard his treasure and their ghosts still haunt the buccaneer's booty.

And yet, for all of the cruelty of Blackbeard and his fellow buccaneers, it still seems impossible not to admire their cunning and ingenuity. Perhaps one of the reasons that piracy still grips the imagination is because pirates are still alive and definitely kicking.

One hundred years after the buccaneers were crushed, another murderous bunch came to power in the east, operating with the same cruelty and viciousness. Eventually they too were hunted down and for a time the seas were quiet again. But, piracy will never die out and today there is a pirate attack every three days in the Straits of Malacca, between Malaysia and Indonesia.

Piracy seems to be here to stay so maybe it's wise to be on the alert when you're next on holiday and see a ship pulling up. Its crew are looking a bit ragged and you don't recognize the flag they're flying. Of course, it's a crazy idea – they couldn't be pirates, could they?

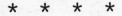

PIRATE TIMELINE

250 BC–AD 250 Pirates terrorize the Mediterranean, attacking the Roman empire.

75 BC Gang of Mediterranean pirates make a big mistake – they try to take Julius Caesar hostage. After he has been freed, he has the pirates killed.

AD 780–1050 Viking pirates attack the North Sea, Atlantic Ocean and Baltic and Black Seas.

1060–1500 Medieval pirates attack the North Sea, Irish Sea and Atlantic Ocean.

1300–1800 Corsairs (including Barbary and Christian) active in the Mediterranean. The different types were enemies of each other.

1500–1750 Buccaneers active in the Caribbean and the American coasts.

1553–1554 François le Clerc (*Jambe de bois*) active – one of the few real-life peg-legged pirates.

June 1692 Port Royal (most famous pirate safe-haven) is destroyed by an earthquake which causes a tidal wave to sweep over the town.

1700–1920 Pirates on junks operate in the Indian Ocean, South China Sea and the Straits of Malacca.

1710s	Blackbeard reaches height of his and his crew's power.
1717–1718	Blackbeard and crew terrorize the Carolinas' coasts, in the United States.
1718	Blackbeard threatens to set port of Charleston alight if he isn't sent a much-needed medical chest immediately. He gets the chest.
November 21st **1718**	Blackbeard caught and killed.
1719	Christopher Condent and his crew wreak havoc in the Red Sea.
1720	Captain Edward England makes successful attacks all over the Indian Ocean but is killed by his crew for 'going soft'.
November 1720	'Calico Jack' killed by a British privateer in the Bahamas.
1720s	Edward Low ravages America's east coast, and makes a man eat his own ear.
1769	One recorded instance of walking the plank.
1807	'Madame Cheng' (Qing Er Sou) becomes most fearsome pirate in the South Seas.
Today	There are still regular pirate attacks in the Straits of Malacca off the Malaysian coast...

GLOSSARY

Articles	Pirate rules
Bilge-water	Dirty water that collects inside a ship
Booty	Stolen goods
Broadside	A volley of shots
Buccaneer	Another name for a pirate
Cannon	A large gun on wheels
Cat o' nine tails	A type of knotted leather whip
Cargo	The contents of a ship
Colony	A settlement in a foreign country
Cutlass	A kind of sword
Davy Jones's locker	Nickname for the sea as a grave for drowned sailors
Dhow	A kind of Arab ship with triangular sails
Doubloon	A gold Spanish coin
Galleon	A large Spanish sailing ship
Galley	A warship with oars and sails
Hold	The part of the ship where the cargo is stored
Hull	The outer shell of the ship
Junk	A kind of Chinese ship

Logbook	A kind of diary recording a ship's voyage
Merchant ship	A ship carrying goods for trading
Pirate	Someone who robs other ships and coastal settlements for any type of goods they can find there
Plantation	Large estate growing crops such as cotton, tobacco or sugar
Plunder	Another word for stolen goods
Privateer	Someone licensed to rob ships by the king or queen
Ransom	A price to pay for the release of a captive
Rum	A kind of alcoholic drink
Ship's biscuit	Special kind of hard biscuit taken to sea for sailors to eat
Sloop	A kind of fast sailing ship with one mast
Treasure	Valuable goods
Yardarm	The horizontal bar supporting the sail